Four Seasons

with the

Bread Machine Baker

Four Seasons

with the

Bread Machine Baker

MORE THAN 130 NEW RECIPES
FOR EVERY OCCASION

Elizabeth M. Harbison

GRAMERCY BOOKS
NEW YORK

This 2001 edition is published by Gramercy Books™,
an imprint of Random House Value Publishing, Inc.
280 Park Avenue, New York, N.Y. 10017.

Gramercy Books™ and design are trademarks of
Random House Value Publishing, Inc.

Random House
New York • Toronto • London • Sydney • Auckland
http://www.randomhouse.com/

Library of Congress Cataloging-in-Publication Data

Harbison, Elizabeth M.
    Four seasons with the bread machine baker / Elizabeth M. Harbison.
        p. cm.
    ISBN 0-517-16298-9 (hardcover)
        1. Bread. 2. Automatic bread machines. I. Title.

TX769 .H292 2001
641.8'15—dc21   00-047657

Printed and bound in the United States of America

9 8 7 6 5 4 3 2 1

Acknowledgments

I would like to thank my mother, Connie Atkins McShulskis, for her help in creating and testing these recipes.

Also thanks to Scout, who did so much to help make my life easier while I was working on this book and welcoming a new baby into the family at the same time.

Thanks to John, Paige and Jack Harbison for being the best family a girl could ask for!

Contents

Introduction   *ix*
Tips for Using this Book *xi*

Winter Breads   *1*
SAVORY   *3*
SWEET   *20*

Spring Breads   *37*
SAVORY   *39*
SWEET   *60*

Summer Breads   *71*
SAVORY   *73*
SWEET   *92*

Autumn Breads   *105*
SAVORY   *107*
SWEET   *130*

Index   *145*

Introduction

This book came about because, after the publication of my first bread machine book, *The Bread Machine Baker*, I continued to experiment with the then-new concept of a bread machine. If you're new to bread machines now, let me give you a brief introduction: bread machines knead, shape, rise and bake your bread for you all in one pan, with no more effort on your part than putting the ingredients in. Sound hokey? It's not. This is essentially hand-made bread, created in a machine. Each machine contains a non-stick bread pan with a paddle in the bottom; when you put the ingredients in and push start, the paddle kneads the dough for about 20 minutes (depending on the cycle), mimicking the stretching, pulling, and folding of the dough that you would do by hand. The machine then stops kneading and heats slightly, to make a nice environment for rising. At the end of the rise cycle, the paddle goes again to "punch down" the loaf. Depending on the cycle, it will either rest and knead again, or go straight into the last rise. At this point the machine heats to baking temperature, and bakes the loaf according to the size and how dark you have said you want the crust.

What you end up with is pretty much what you would have gotten after kneading, rising, punching down, shaping and baking it all by hand. The advantage, however, is that it is much less time- and energy-consuming. Plus you can set the timer to have your fresh-baked bread ready when you wake up in the morning. Finally, the machine can make some breads that have such loose, sticky doughs that they would be difficult or impossible to make by hand.

This last point is the most exciting one to me. If I were making bread by hand, I would be nervous about experimenting with unusual ingredients or proportions, but a bread machine seems to have a little magic to it. I have been amazed to find that almost everything I try works, no matter how crazy it seems (see "Chips and Beer Bread" and "Cap'n Crunch Bread"). The bread machine is a remarkably versatile (and forgiving) thing!

So that's the main reason for this book: I have created and modified so many new and unique recipes that I simply had to collect them all in one new volume. Although I have a few reliable standards in white, wheat, and cheese breads, I have added fun and fabulous new taste combinations. I can safely say you won't see most of these recipes, or their like, in any other book!

After collecting all my new recipes, I was then challenged with how to present them. Was an Apple Walnut Loaf a fruit bread or a nut/seed bread? Was Bleu Cheese Whole Wheat Bread a cheese bread or wheat bread? They could have gone either way. But one thing I did know was that I ate a lot of the Apple Walnut Bread in the autumn, when apples were plentiful and when the cooler air just seemed to scream for a warming cinnamon scent. As I looked over the recipes, I saw that many of them fell easily into seasons, either because they called for seasonal ingredients (sun-dried tomato and basil in the summer, pumpkin in the autumn) or because they were holiday breads (traditional Christmas loaves, Easter loaves, etc.), or just because heavier breads seemed better suited to colder weather while lighter breads seemed right for summer. However, this is not to say you can't enjoy Cranberry Pumpkin bread all year long—I served it at Easter just this year!

It's all about experimenting, using the ingredients you have on hand and the tastes you are in the mood for, and trying something new. The recipes in this book should satisfy on all counts. I hope you enjoy each one as much as I have!

Elizabeth Harbison
http://www.ElizabethHarbison.com

Tips for Using This Book

Rise to the occasion—it is not necessary to proof yeast for these recipes—with a bread machine, you just throw the dry yeast into the bread pan along with the rest of the ingredients. However, bad yeast will ruin a loaf and give you a big hockey puck. If you suspect your yeast may be dead or inactive, proof it separately before using it in a recipe by adding a teaspoon or two of sugar to some warm water and sprinkling a teaspoon of yeast on top. Wait five minutes. If it gets foamy and bubbly, it's good yeast (though you'll still have to throw away your proofing experiment and use dry yeast for the recipe). If nothing happens, or the yeast seems to sink to the bottom of the cup, throw it out and get new yeast. As for which kind of yeast to use—compressed fresh or active dry—it's up to you. I use one of one of those little square bricks of fresh yeast in place of about 2 t of active dry. I do not recommend using rapid rise yeast; all of these recipes are designed for traditional active dry or fresh.

Add the ingredients according to your manufacturer's instructions—some bread machines come with instructions to add the liquid first, others say to add the dry ingredients first. I have never noticed a difference either way (after all, it's kneaded right away anyhow, unless you are using a timed cycle), and it certainly does not matter to my recipes, but just in case it does matter to your machine, please follow the manufacturer's guidelines.

These recipes are for 1 lb. loaves, but they can be increased—to make 2 lb. loaves from these recipes, simply double the proportions (2 cups of flour becomes 4 cups, 1-1/2 cups of milk becomes 3 cups, and so forth). To make 1-1/2 lb. loaves, increase all of the ingredients by one half (2 cups of flour becomes 3 cups, 1-1/2 cups of milk becomes 2-1/4 cups, and so forth). It's that simple.

Not all ingredients are created equal—every ingredient you will use for these recipes has its own variables that can make the bread work or not work. Riper bananas compensate for more liquid than greener ones, and sometimes you cannot tell how juicy an apple, peach, pear, etc. is going to be. Sometimes even flour that has been sitting on a supermarket shelf for a very long time ends up requiring slightly more liquid than fresher flour. For that reason, I tested each recipe several times and in more than one machine, and have tried to come up with a good "medium" of proportions. Even so, there may occasionally be discrepancies between the ingredients you use and the ones I used. If you have any questions feel free to look in the machine while it is kneading and make sure the dough is smooth and elastic, and just a little sticky to the touch. If it's too dry, add a tablespoon of liquid at a time until it's the right consistency; if it's too wet, add a tablespoon of flour at a time.

There's flour and then there's flour—although you can use all-purpose flour in place of bread flour in any of these recipes, I prefer bread flour because it makes for a better rise and thus a lighter loaf. Basically the difference between the two is that bread flour is a hard wheat flour with high gluten, whereas all-purpose flour is a mixture of hard wheat and soft wheat (which is low gluten). Bread flour is available in virtually any grocery store; you will find it alongside all-purpose flour. If you would rather mail order, King Arthur also makes wonderful bread flours and even bread machine flour—you can find them at www.KingArthurflour.com or by calling 1-800-827-6836.

Not everyone likes eggs—as I mentioned in my introduction, I was sometimes amazed at how forgiving the bread machine could be as I experimented with various ingredients. While the recipes have only been tested as printed, you can usually safely omit an egg and replace it with 1/4 cup of milk or water. By the same token, you can replace milk with water if you do not like dairy products. You may also reduce the salt down to about 1/4 teaspoon in most recipes without problems to the loaf. However, bear in mind that every loaf needs salt, as well as some kind of natural sweetener (honey, sugar, brown sugar, molasses, but *never* artificial sweeteners like saccharine or aspartame) to regulate the action of the yeast.

Other substitutions—I have noted several of these recipes "Dairy-Free" even though they call for butter or margarine. If you wish to prepare them Dairy-Free, obviously use margarine instead of butter. You may also use low-cholesterol egg replacements instead of eggs, but all of them are different and you should follow the manufacturer's instructions on replacing eggs in recipes. Then, as always, take a peek at your dough while its kneading to make sure it's the right consistency.

Herbs—unless otherwise noted, I like to use dried herbs in my breads because they're easier to work with and the taste is more predictable (and, I think, better in breads). If you would rather use fresh herbs, though, please feel free. Note that fresh herbs are not as strong as dried, and you'll have to experiment with proportions—I'd usually use 1/4 cup of loosely packed basil leaves in place of 2 teaspoons of dried. Likewise, you may dry your own fresh herbs by placing them on a paper towel in the microwave and heat on high for 30 seconds.

Sweet Breads—The sugar in many sweet breads—especially chocolate sweet breads—makes the bread get very brown and sometimes burn, especially if your machine does not have a "sweet" cycle. It's a good idea to cook them on "light" or "medium" cycle and check them towards the end.

Sometimes things go wrong—whether it's altitude, ingredient variability, or the alignment of the planets, sometimes things just don't work out. Sometimes there doesn't seem to be any explanation for it, but usually there is: A loaf that sinks in the middle, is not cooked through, or one that collapses probably had too much liquid. Next time adjust your liquid to dry proportions. A loaf that is so short and dense that it's inedible, either rose too high, too fast and collapsed (in which case you would want to take away a little of the sweetener and/or add a pinch more salt to slow the yeast rising), or did not rise enough in the first place (either because of too much salt, not enough sweetener, or dead yeast C for the latter, proof a bit of your yeast once a week, as outlined above, just to make sure it's still active). A loaf that rises too high needs just a little less sugar and yeast and/or a little more salt next time around (though I've always liked those super tall loaves). If you consistently find that your bread does not rise as much as you'd like— or if you would rather just buy all-purpose flour and give it some extra oomph yourself—you may buy dough conditioners and powdered glutens to make the yeast work better. One of the best sources is, again, King Arthur Flour Company (see information above). I also recommend Lora Brody's dough enhancers (in regular or sourdough flavor!), which you can find at www.LoraBrody.com.

Winter Breads

In the cold, dark days of winter, we turn to

heavier, more satisfying breads: sweet

dark chocolates, chewy whole grains, savory

cheese and warming spice breads are a

few of the offerings here for

your winter table.

Mexicali Beer Bread (Dairy-Free)

*You may prefer to leave the green chilies out of this recipe,
or, if you're adventurous, add jalapeños.*

7/8 c light beer such as Corona (unless you like the stronger flavor of a deeper ale)	2 t mild green chilies
	1/2 t chili powder
	1/4 t cumin
1 T butter or margarine	2 c bread flour
1 t salt	2 t yeast
1 T sugar	

Add the ingredients to your machine according to the manufacturer's instructions.

Use a regular/white, light, or rapid bread cycle.

Golden Egg Bread

*This is such a simple loaf that it may appear to be too plain at first,
but if you're looking for a nice loaf to compliment any
meal and which can be prepared on a rapid or
regular cycle, this is the one for you.*

1/2 c buttermilk	1 t salt
3 T water	2 c bread flour
2 T dry milk powder	4 t sugar
1 egg	2 t yeast
4 t butter or margarine	

Add the ingredients to your machine according to the manufacturer's instructions.

Use a regular/white, light, or rapid bread cycle.

Semolina Corn Bread

*Don't be discouraged by what looks like a very sticky dough
at first—it comes together shortly before the
end of the first kneading cycle.*

*If you want to use cottage cheese instead of ricotta, bear in mind that
it makes a difference in the moisture content, so you might want
to start with 3/4 cup of milk to 1 cup of cottage cheese
and add more milk by the tablespoonful if necessary.*

1 c milk	1/2 c semolina flour
1 c part-skim ricotta cheese	1/2 c corn meal
1 t salt	1 T sugar
1-1/2 c + 2 T bread flour	3 t yeast

Add the ingredients to your machine according to the manufacturer's
instructions.

Use a regular, light, or rapid bread cycle.

Champagne and Cheddar Bread

*If you've ever wondered what to do with that leftover
champagne after a party, here's a yummy answer.*

3/4 c flat champagne

1 T + 1 t light vegetable oil

2-1/4 c bread flour

1/2 c shredded sharp cheddar
cheese

1/2 t salt

1 t sugar

2 t yeast

Add the ingredients to your machine according to the manufacturer's
instructions.

Use a regular/white, light, or rapid bread cycle.

Hot Hot Hot Jalapeño Bread

Here's a warming bread for cold winter nights!

*I keep a small jar of sliced jalapeño peppers in my refrigerator and,
having a somewhat faint palate, usually use just one or two slices
for this whole loaf, though you may use up to 3 tablespoons
of it. Also, add the peppers at the indicator beep if you
want them to remain more intact—I like the flavor
mixed well in the bread so I add it at the beginning.*

1 c milk	1 t salt
2 T butter or margarine	1 t ground black pepper
3 T chopped jalapenos	4 t sugar
2 c bread flour	2 t yeast

Add the ingredients to your machine according to the manufacturer's instructions. Or, if you prefer, add the jalapeños at the indicator beep. Use a regular/white, light, or rapid bread cycle.

Oat O's Cereal Bread

Use Cheerios or the generic equivalent for this bread.

1 c milk

1 egg

2 t butter or margarine

1 t salt

.2 c bread flour

2 c crunchy oat "O's" cereal

2 T sugar

2-3 t yeast

Add the ingredients to your machine according to the manufacturer's instructions.

Bake on a regular/white, light, or rapid cycle

Swedish Hoska

*This Swedish holiday bread, adapted for the machine by Connie Atkins,
is best eaten the first day...not usually a problem since it's so tasty
it will be gobbled up! It's especially nice when spread
with icing glaze made from 1/4 c confectioners
sugar and 2 t orange juice.*

1/3 c scalded milk	1 t grated fresh orange or
1/4 c water	lemon peel (or 1/4 t dried)
1 T butter or margarine	2 t yeast
1 egg	2 T raisins
2 c bread flour	2 T craisins
2 T sugar	2 T dried cherries
1 t salt	1/4 c slivered almonds

Add the ingredients to your machine, except raisins, craisins, dried cherries, and almonds, according to the manufacturer's instructions. Add the fruit and nuts at the indicator beep.

Bake on a sweet or regular/white cycle.

Double Mustard Onion Beer Bread

*I like to use a mild domestic beer for this recipe, so as not to
overwhelm the flavor of the bread by competing with
the strong flavors of mustard and onion.*

*It's also important to note that, for reasons I cannot figure out, the
beer can be a real variable in the consistency of this dough.
Take a peek after the dough has been kneading for 10 minutes or so.
It should be sticky but not the consistency of cake batter. If it
appears too loose to you, add 1/4 cup of flour, then about
a tablespoon at a time until you have a sticky,
ball-shaped, dough.*

3/4 c mild beer	3/4 t salt
1 small onion, chopped (about	2-1/4 c bread flour
1/2 cup)	1 T sugar
2 T prepared mustard	1/2 t mustard powder
1 T butter or margarine	2–3 t yeast

Add the ingredients to your machine according to the manufacturer's
instructions.

Bake on a regular/white, light, or rapid cycle.

Light Rye with Cheddar and Fennel

This is wonderful with a strong, spicy soup, such as mulligatawny.

3/4 c water	1 t salt
1 T molasses	1 t fennel seed
1 T canola oil	1/2 c grated sharp cheddar
3/4 c rye flour	cheese
1-3/4 c bread flour	2 t yeast

Add the ingredients to your machine according to the manufacturer's instructions.

Bake on a regular/white, light, or rapid cycle.

Tangy Rye Bread (Dairy-Free)

*The trick to this bread is in chopping the onion
very fine in your food processor. There should be no large
onion chunks in the finished bread.*

1 c water	1 t onion salt
1 T light vegetable oil	1/3 c finely chopped onion
1 T honey	1 c rye flour
1 T molasses	2 c bread flour
1 t plain instant coffee crystals	2 t yeast
1 T Dutch processed cocoa	

Add the ingredients to your machine according to the manufacturer's
instructions.

Bake on a regular/white, light, or medium cycle.

This recipe may be prepared on a timed cycle.

South Carolina Rice Bread

I have no idea how old this recipe is. The original came from the cousin of a dear friend of mine, and her report was that her mother had made it back as far as she could remember. In any event, it makes for a very nice white bread, perfect for toasting or for sandwiches.

2 c milk	1 T butter or margarine
2 c cooked white rice (I like Basmati, but you can use any)	3/4 t salt
	1 T sugar
1 egg	2 c bread flour
2 t white vinegar	2 t active dry yeast

Add the ingredients to your machine according to the manufacturer's instructions.

Bake on a regular/white, light, medium, or rapid cycle.

Semi-Wheat Sally Lunn

Here's another favorite of mine!

Some people mistakenly believe that scalding milk is an old-fashioned way of killing bacteria, and therefore unnecessary in recipes which use modern pasteurized milk. In fact, scalding milk brings out more sweetness and allows the yeast to work even better.

3/4 c milk, scalded	3/4 t salt
2 eggs	1-1/2 c bread flour
2 T butter or margarine	2/3 c whole wheat flour
1 T brown sugar	2 t yeast

Add the ingredients to your machine according to the manufacturer's instructions.

Bake on a regular/white, regular/wheat, light, medium or rapid cycle.

Oatmeal Molasses Bread (Dairy-Free)

*Over the years, I've found several variations of this bread
that I enjoy, but this is one of the simplest.*

3/4 to 1 c water

3 T light vegetable oil

3 T molasses

2 c bread flour

1/2 c old-fashioned rolled oats

1 t salt

2 t yeast

Add the ingredients to your machine according to the manufacturer's
instructions.

Bake on a regular, light, medium or rapid cycle.

This recipe may be prepared on a timed cycle.

Chocolate Oatmeal Bread

*It took a lot of experimenting, but I finally perfected this awesome,
rich bread. It's heavenly, either by itself or spread with
butter or margarine, peanut butter, or Nutella.*

3/4 c water

2 eggs

2 t vanilla extract

2 t vinegar

2 T butter or margarine

2 t honey

1/3 c dry milk powder

2 c + 2 T bread flour

1/3 c + 3 T rolled oats

1/3 c brown sugar

1/3 c Dutch processed cocoa

1/2 t salt

1 t baking soda

3 t yeast

Add the ingredients to your machine according to the manufacturer's
instructions.

Use a regular, white, wheat, or rapid bread cycle.

Sesame Tahini Bread (Dairy-Free)

*Sesame oil is one of my favorite ingredients for just about anything,
so I've added it here, but if you don't have it or don't like
the taste, you may replace it with plain vegetable oil. It really
is a tasty, nutritious bread, perfect spread with peanut butter
or tahini. Likewise, you may use any plain milk
instead of the rice milk, if you prefer.*

1 c rice milk	1 c bread flour
1 t light vegetable oil	1 c whole wheat flour
1 t sesame oil	1/4 c quick oats
1/2 t almond extract	1/4 c sugar
2 T sesame tahini	2 t yeast
1 t salt	

Add the ingredients to your machine according to the manufacturer's
instructions.

Use a sweet, regular/white, light, or rapid bread cycle.

This bread can be prepared on a timed cycle.

Champagne "Sourdough" Bread

It isn't essential to use quality champagne for this bread—it's one of the only exceptions I can think of for the "don't cook with any wine you wouldn't like to drink" rule. This is a dense loaf with an elegant flavor—perfect for salmon spread.

3/4 c champagne	1/2 t salt
1 large egg	1 T honey
1 T butter or margarine	3 t yeast, divided
2-1/2 c bread flour, divided	

At least 12 hours before you're ready to bake the bread, put the champagne, 2 t yeast, and 3/4 c bread flour into the machine and let it mix for a few minutes. Then leave it overnight or for 12 hours, to form a sponge.

After that, add the remaining ingredients and bake on a regular/white or rapid cycle.

Texas Beer Bread

You may choose to shred both cheeses, and add them all at the beginning. This is convenient, and makes one, smoothly cheesy loaf. However, if you add cubes of Monterey Jack cheese at the indicator beep (about half an hour into the knead cycle), you'll have lovely pockets of gooey cheese.

1 c flat beer	3 cloves garlic, minced
1 T butter or margarine	2 c bread flour
4 oz shredded sharp cheddar	1 T sugar
cheese	1 t salt
3 oz cubed Jack cheese	2 t yeast

Add the ingredients to your machine according to the manufacturer's instructions.

Use a regular/white, light, or rapid bread cycle.

This bread can be prepared on a timed cycle.

Chocolate Chip Cocoa Bread

*This is lovely with a cup of hot chocolate
on a cold night.*

*Add the chocolate chips one minute before the
end of the kneading cycle.*

1 c milk	1/4 c unsweetened cocoa
1 egg	powder
1/2 t almond extract	1/2 c chocolate chips
1 t vanilla	3/4 c sugar
2 T butter or margarine	1 t salt
2 c bread flour	3 scant t yeast

Add all the ingredients to your machine, except the chocolate chips, according to the manufacturer's instructions. Add the chocolate chips at the very end of the kneading cycle, *not at the indicator beep.*

Use a sweet, regular, light, or rapid bread cycle.

Rum–Soaked Currant Bread (Dairy-Free)

I like to use Captain Morgan's Spiced Rum for this warming, winter recipe. Just use enough to cover the currants. Any leftover rum may be used for hot buttered rum!

Because this makes a low, dense bread, you might prefer to "fluff it up" by using a teaspoon of wheat gluten, but my family likes it dense. It's very flavorful.

3/4 c water	1 t salt
1 c currants, soaked in spiced rum overnight, then drained	2 T sugar
	2 t butter or margarine
3 T rum from the drained currants	1/8 t ground ginger or pumpkin pie spice
2 c bread flour	3 t yeast

Add all the ingredients to your machine, except the soaked currants, according to the manufacturer's instructions. Add the currants at the indicator beep.

Bake on a sweet, regular, light, or rapid cycle.

You may also prepare this bread on a timed cycle, if you don't mind adding the currants in the beginning and having them thoroughly incorporated into the bread.

Walnut Date Bread (Dairy-Free)

*You may use regular raisins in place of
the golden raisins in this recipe, if you prefer.*

7/8 c water

1-1/2 T butter or margarine

1-1/3 c bread flour

2/3 c whole wheat flour

2 T wheat germ

1/2 t ground cinnamon

dash ground ginger

3/4 t salt

2 T brown sugar

2 t yeast

1/2 c chopped dates

1/4 c raisins

3 T chopped walnuts

Add all the ingredients to your machine, except the dates, raisins, and walnuts, according to the manufacturer's instructions. Add the dates and walnuts at the indicator beep.

Use a sweet, regular, light, or rapid bread cycle.

This bread can be prepared on a timed cycle.

Cranberry Orange Bread

*This is, in my humble opinion, one of the most underrated
flavor combinations, a real knock-out.*

*Of course this bread can be prepared in any season, but something about the
spicy, orange-y scent is very festive and makes me think of the winter holidays.*

1/3 c milk	pinch mace
1/2 c orange juice	1/4 c Craisins or dried
1 egg	cranberries
4 t butter or margarine	2 t yeast
2 - 1/4 c bread flour	1/4 c powdered sugar
1 t salt	enough orange juice to make
1 t orange zest	a paste with the powdered
1/4 t nutmeg	sugar (about 2 T)
1/4 t ginger	1/2 t orange rind
1/4 t cinnamon	

Combine the 1/4 cup of powdered sugar, 2 Tablespoons (approx.) of
orange juice, and 1/2 teaspoon of orange rind in a small bowl and set
aside. This will be the glaze for the finished bread.

Add the remaining ingredients to your machine, except for the
dried cranberries, in the order suggested by the manufacturer. Add the
cranberries at the indicator beep.

Bake on a sweet or regular/white bread cycle.

When the bread is done, remove it from the pan and paint on the
powdered sugar/orange glaze. Allow to cool slightly, then serve.

Pecan and Raisin Wheat Bread

If the pecans you use for this recipe are salted, omit the 1/2 teaspoon of salt from this recipe. Also bear in mind that you may omit the raisins if you don't like them. I often prepare this as a simple Pecan Wheat Bread.

3/4 c water	1 T butter or margarine
1-3/4 c bread flour	1 T dry milk
1/4 c whole wheat flour	2 t yeast
1/2 t salt	1/4 c pecan pieces
2 T sugar	1/4 c raisins

Add all the ingredients to your machine, except the raisins and pecans, in the order specified by the manufacturer. Add the raisins and pecans at the indicator beep.

Use a regular, white, wheat, light, or rapid bread cycle.

This bread can be prepared on a timed cycle.

Cinnamon Nut Bread (Dairy-Free)

*This makes a very high, light loaf with a crisp crust.
It's not terribly sweet unless you top it with a
sweet spread (like cinnamon and butter!)*

*This recipe originally called for walnuts, but I prefer the milder
sweetness of pecans. You may, however, use any nut
you want, or you may omit the nuts altogether.*

3/4 c + 2 T water	2-1/4 c bread flour
1 T oil	1 t cinnamon
1/2 t white vinegar	2 t yeast
2 T brown sugar	1/4 c raisins
1/4 c applesauce	1/3 c pecans, or other nuts
1 t salt	

Add all the ingredients to your machine, except the raisins and nuts, in the order specified by the manufacturer. Add the raisins and nuts at the indicator beep.

Use a sweet, regular/white, light, or rapid bread cycle.

This bread can be prepared on a timed cycle.

Sweet Orange Bread

This is a delicious bread to make with the juice of ripe navel or Valencia oranges of January and February, though you may use orange juice from concentrate if you prefer. Marmalade makes an excellent topping.

When zesting the orange, be careful not to get any of the bitter white pulp in the mix.

3/4 c orange juice

1/2 t orange extract

1 egg

2 t butter or margarine

2 c bread flour

3 T granulated sugar

1/2 t salt

4 t orange zest

2 t yeast

Add the ingredients to your machine according to the manufacturer's instructions.

Cook on a sweet, regular/white, light or rapid cycle.

Maple Oatmeal Breakfast Bread (Dairy-Free)

*Send the family off in the morning with something substantial in their
bellies with this simple, filling bread. Or, make the best French
Toast you ever had by cutting thick slices of this bread, dipping them
in a mixture of 3 eggs, 1-1/2 cups of milk, 2 teaspoons
vanilla extract, 1 teaspoon of cinnamon, 3 tablespoons of sugar,
and then cooking them on a hot waffle iron!*

1 c water	2 c bread flour
1 T light vegetable oil	3/4 c old-fashioned rolled oats
1/3 c maple syrup	2 t yeast
1 t salt	

Add the ingredients to your machine according to the manufacturer's
instructions.

Use a sweet, regular/white, light, or rapid bread cycle.

This bread can be prepared on a timed cycle.

Golden Raisin Loaf (Dairy-Free)

*You may use regular raisins in place of the golden
raisins in this recipe, if you prefer.*

1 c water	2 T brown sugar
1-1/2 T butter or margarine	1/2 t ground cinnamon
3/4 t salt	dash ground ginger
1-1/3 c bread flour	2 t yeast
2/3 c whole wheat flour	1/2 c golden raisins
2 T wheat germ	

Add all the ingredients to your machine, except the raisins, according
to the manufacturer's instructions. Add the raisins at the indicator beep.

Use a regular, light, fruit/nut, or rapid bread cycle.

This bread can be prepared on a timed cycle.

Chocolate Almond Bread

*This bread is a knock out, delicious with your morning coffee.
I've used the timer cycle successfully for up to eight hours
in advance, but I wouldn't want to go much
longer than that because of the eggs.*

*If you don't have a "sweet bread" cycle on your machine,
either bake this on light, or stop the baking five minutes early.
Something I also do sometimes is open the machine several
times during baking, to cool the air off inside.*

3/4 c milk	1/4 c sugar
2 T buttermilk (or regular milk with a dash of lemon juice)	1/3 c Dutch processed cocoa
1 t vanilla extract	1/2 t salt
3/4 t almond extract	3/4 t cinnamon
3 egg yolks	1 t orange peel
1/4 c butter or margarine	1 T brown sugar
2 c bread flour, divided	2 t yeast

Put the milk and buttermilk into a saucepan and bring it to a boil. Add 1/2 cup of the bread flour and stir into a thick paste. Let the mixture cool to room temperature, then put it in the bread machine pan and add the remaining ingredients.

Bake on a light or sweet bread cycle.

Dark Cocoa Bread

This is not as sweet as the "Chocolate Almond Bread." In fact, you may like to use this for savory sandwiches and spreads.

1 c milk

1 egg

1/2 t vanilla extract

2 T butter or margarine

1 t salt

2 c bread flour

1/4 c Dutch processed cocoa

1/2 c sugar

1 T (3 scant t) yeast

Add the ingredients to your machine according to the manufacturer's instructions.

Use a regular, sweet, light, or rapid bread cycle.

Craisin Oatmeal Bread (Dairy-Free)

If you're not as big a fan of Craisins as I am, you can use raisins, currants, or dried, reconstituted cranberries for this recipe.

1 c water	1-1/2 c bread flour
1 T light vegetable oil	3/4 c old-fashioned rolled oats
1 T molasses	2 t yeast
1-1/2 t salt	1/4 c loosely packed Craisins

Boil the 1 cup of water, then mix it with the oatmeal and allow it to cool some (until it's not unbearably hot to the touch.)

Add all the ingredients to your machine, including the oatmeal mixture but omitting the Craisins, in the order suggested by the manufacturer, and push "start." Add the Craisins at the indicator beep.

Bake on a regular or light cycle.

This recipe may be prepared on a timed cycle.

Chocolate Spiced Rum Babka

*Traditional Polish Babka is flavored with plain rum and
contains no chocolate, but this variation makes a delicious
bread for either dessert or with morning coffee.*

*I've used the timer cycle as long as eight hours in advance,
but I wouldn't want to go much longer than that because of the eggs.*

*If you don't have a sweet bread cycle on your machine,
remember to check and stop the baking five minutes
early to prevent burning.*

3/4 c + 1 T milk	1/3 c Dutch processed cocoa
1 T spiced rum	1/2 t salt
1 t vanilla extract	3/4 t cinnamon
3 egg yolks	1/8 t allspice
3 T butter or margarine	1 T brown sugar
2 c + 2 T bread flour	2 t yeast
4 T sugar	

Add the ingredients to your machine according to the manufacturer's
instructions.

Bake on a light or sweet bread cycle.

Cinnamon Cream Bread

This may strike you as a lot of cinnamon, but it doesn't overwhelm the flavor of this bread. It does, however, keep the yeast from puffing the dough very high, so you end up with a dense loaf.

3/4 c + 2 t half and half	2 t cinnamon
3 T butter or margarine	1/2 t salt
2 c bread flour	2–3 t yeast
3 T sugar	

Add the ingredients to your machine according to the manufacturer's instructions.

Use a regular, light, sweet, or rapid bread cycle.

This bread can be prepared on a timed cycle.

Holiday Chocolate Mint Bread

Try this one plain with minted hot cocoa—yum!

3/4 c + 4 t milk	1/3 c unsweetened cocoa
3/4 t mint extract	powder
3 egg yolks	2 t salt
4 T butter or margarine	1 t lemon peel
2 c bread flour, divided	1 T brown sugar
4 T sugar	2 t yeast

Put the milk into a saucepan and bring it to a boil. Add 1/2 cup of the bread flour and stir it into a thick paste. Let the mixture cool to room temperature, then put it in the bread machine pan and add the remaining ingredients.

Bake on a regular/white, light or sweet bread cycle.

French Sweet Bread with Rum Butter

Because of the alcohol in the rum butter, children or those
with alcohol problems should enjoy this bread plain.

1/2 c milk	1 t salt
1/3 c water	2 T sugar
2 T light vegetable oil	2 c bread flour
1 egg	2 t yeast
1/2 t vanilla extract	1/2 c raisins
1/2 t almond extract	1/4 c almond slivers

Add the ingredients to your machine, except the raisins and almonds, according to the manufacturer's instructions. Add the raisins and almonds at the indicator beep.

Bake on a sweet or regular/white cycle.

When the bread is done, top slices with Rum Butter (below).

RUM BUTTER

1/2 c butter or margarine, at room temperature	2 c sifted confectioners sugar
	1 T rum

Cream the butter or margarine with the sugar, and blend in the rum.

Cinnamon Chip Bread

This is a variation of a bread that was in the King Arthur Flour catalog.
It's just as good as it sounds; maybe even better. In my opinion,
the King Arthur cinnamon chips are the best (you can get them from
the web site, www.kingarthurflour.com), but you can also
find cinnamon chips at the grocery store.

1/2 c water	2 T sugar
1 egg	1/2 t baking powder
4 t butter or margarine	2 T nonfat dry milk powder
1 t vanilla extract	2 c bread flour
1 t cinnamon	2 t yeast
1/2 t ginger	3/4 c cinnamon chips
3/4 t salt	

Add all the ingredients to your machine, except the cinnamon chips, according to the manufacturer's instructions. Add the cinnamon chips at the indicator beep.

Bake on a sweet, regular, or rapid cycle.

This recipe may be prepared on a timed cycle, up to eight hours in advance.

Spring Breads

As the weather grows warmer, we look for lighter breads: sweet and savory Easter breads from around the world, tangy citrus breads, sweet fruit breads and light wheats are included for your spring picnic baskets and tables.

Italian Peasant Bread

*Here's a yummy, tender white bread that goes
with just about anything.*

3/4 c water	1 t salt
2 t butter or margarine	1 t sugar
2 T nonfat milk powder	2 t yeast
2 c bread flour	

Add the ingredients to your machine according to the manufacturer's instructions.

Bake on a regular, light, or rapid cycle.

This bread can be prepared on a timed cycle.

Indian Molasses Bread

*This is a nutritious bread without the heaviness of
regular whole wheat, which makes it a good
choice for white bread fanatics.*

1/2 c milk, scalded	1/2 c whole wheat flour
1/2 c water	1/2 c cornmeal
1 T butter or margarine	1 t salt
2 T molasses	1/2 t cinnamon
2 T brown sugar	dash of nutmeg
1 c bread flour	2 t yeast

Add the ingredients to your machine according to the manufacturer's
instructions.

Bake on a regular/white, wheat or light cycle

Dill Bread

This has long been a favorite of mine. Because different brands of farmer's cheese have different moisture contents, peek at the dough while it's kneading to make sure it's a smooth elastic ball. If it's too crumbly, add a tablespoon of water at a time until it reaches the proper consistency.

1 c farmer's cheese	1 t salt
1/2 c water	1 T dried dill weed
2 eggs	2 T sugar
2 c bread flour	2 t yeast
1/4 t baking soda	

Add the ingredients to your machine according to the manufacturer's instructions.

Bake on a regular, light, or rapid cycle.

Spiced White Bread

Yes, that's cinnamon there! Believe it or not, it works well in this moist, herb-y loaf, and no one will be able to guess what your "secret ingredient" is.

3/4 c + 2 T milk
1/2 c cottage cheese
2 c bread flour
1 t salt
1/2 t dried rosemary
1 t dried parsley

1/2 t dried tarragon
1/4 t cinnamon
1 T sugar
2 t butter or margarine
2 t yeast

Add the ingredients to your machine according to the manufacturer's instructions.

Bake on a regular, light, or rapid cycle.

Garlic Butter Bread (Dairy-Free)

The perfect accompaniment to a lasagne dinner. The fainthearted
may use less garlic but once it's baked into the bread,
the flavor is not as strong as you might expect.

3/4 c water

4 T butter or margarine

2 c bread flour

2 t sugar

1 t salt

5 cloves of fresh garlic, minced

2 t yeast

Add the ingredients to your machine according to the manufacturer's
instructions.

Bake on a regular, light, or rapid cycle.

Honey Mustard Bread

This is a somewhat dense loaf, with a nice domed top.

While you can use your own favorite mustard, I've had great success using two varieties from Harry and David's: Champagne Honey Mustard and Garlic Aioli Mustard.

2 c + 1 T milk

1/4 c chicken broth (or water to which you've added 1 cube of chicken bouillon)

1-1/2 c bread flour

1/2 c whole wheat flour

2 T honey

3 T honey mustard (or 2–3 T plain mustard, depending on your taste)

1 t salt

2–3 t yeast

Add the ingredients to your machine according to the manufacturer's instructions.

Use a regular, light, or rapid bread cycle.

Savory Olive Bread

*This is a variation on a recipe from the back of a Gold Medal
flour bag. I like the flavor and appearance of it withpimiento
olives, but if you prefer you may use plain, pitted olives.*

3/4 c + 2 T water

1 T olive oil

1 egg

1/4 c shredded sharp cheddar
   cheese

2 t salt

1/4 t freshly ground pepper

2 t sugar

2 c + 2 T bread flour

2 t yeast

1/2 c pitted olives, with or
   without pimientos, well drained

Add the ingredients to your machine, except the olives, according to
the manufacturer's instructions. Add the olives at the indicator beep.

Bake on a regular/white, light, or rapid cycle.

You may also prepare this recipe on a timed cycle, up to six hours
in advance. The olives will become integrated into the batter.

Rich Dinner Roll Bread

*This is just delicious with any dinner, from chili to
soup to steak, or simply as buttered toast.*

3/4 c half and half (or milk)	1 t salt
2 egg yolks	1/4 c sugar
3 T butter or margarine	2 t yeast
2 c flour	

Add the ingredients to your machine according to the manufacturer's instructions.

If you like, you can make a glaze of 1 egg yolk and 1 T of milk, and paint it on at the end of the final rise.

Use a regular/white, light, or rapid bread cycle.

1950's Kitchen Bread

A friend gave me this recipe, saying her mother—a real "back-of-the box cook"—used to make this bread for "fancy dinner" nights.

You can substitute Velveeta for the American cheese in this recipe, if you like. It makes for a very cheesy flavor that kids love.

7/8 c buttermilk	1 t salt
2 T butter or margarine	1/4 t garlic powder
1/3 c shredded American cheese	2 c bread flour
1/4 c coarsely chopped onion	1 T sugar
	2 t yeast

Add the ingredients to your machine according to the manufacturer's instructions.

Use a regular, light, or rapid bread cycle.

Almond Blue Cheese Loaf

You may substitute plain milk for the buttermilk if you prefer a less tangy flavored bread.

1 c buttermilk	1 t salt
1 t canola oil	1/4 c crumbled blue cheese
2 c bread flour	1/4 c almond pieces (or slivers)
2 t honey	2 t yeast

Add the ingredients to your machine according to the manufacturer's instructions. You may add the almonds after the indicator beep, if you prefer chunks. I like the flavor incorporated for this loaf.

Use a regular, light, or rapid bread cycle.

Pizza Al Formaggio

This delicious Italian cheese loaf was invented by my mother, Connie Atkins, after she had some Italian cheese bread my godmother brought over from Rome. I tasted both, and this moist, delicious bread beat the genuine Italian one hands down.

1/2 c heavy cream

1/2 c water

1 egg

2 T butter or margarine

1 c Pecorino Romano cheese
  (3/4 c grated + 1/4 c cut
  into 1/2-inch chunks)

2–3 cloves garlic, minced

2 c bread flour

2 T yellow corn meal

1 T sugar

3 scant t yeast

Scald the cream and remove it from the heat. Add the butter or margarine. When the butter is melted, add the water, egg, and cheese, and stir. Put this mixture into the bread pan and add the other ingredients to the machine, except the cheese chunks, according to the manufacturer's instructions. Add the cheese chunks at the indicator beep.

Bake on a regular/white, light, or rapid cycle.

Sharp Cheddar Bread

This is a great staple bread, unbeatable toasted with butter,
for any time you want a nice snack.

7/8 c buttermilk	1 t salt
1/2 c grated extra sharp cheddar	1 T sugar
2 c bread flour	2–3 t yeast
3/4 t baking powder	

Add the ingredients to your machine according to the manufacturer's instructions.

Use a regular/white, light, or rapid bread cycle.

Basil Pepper Feta Loaf

This is a zesty, delicious loaf, that rises high and light.
Delicious hot with butter or spread with basil pesto.

2/3 c + 1 T water

1 egg

1 T sugar

2 c bread flour

1 t salt

1/4 t ground pepper

1/4 c fresh basil, minced (or

2 t dried)

4 oz. feta cheese

2 t yeast

Add the ingredients to your machine according to the manufacturer's instructions.

Bake on a regular/white, light, or rapid cycle

King's Ransom Bread

*My husband decided we should call this "King's Ransom Bread"
when he saw the price of the Stilton I was buying and was
unmoved by my explanation that, in England, Stilton
is considered the "King of Cheeses."*

*This is a nicely textured bread, easy to slice and nice
with dips as an appetizer. If you ask me, it's worth a king's ransom.*

1 c milk	3 T shredded cheddar cheese
1 T butter or margarine	2 c old-fashioned rolled oats
1 egg	2 c + 3 T bread flour
1/2 c crumbled Stilton cheese	2 t yeast

Add the ingredients to your machine according to the manufacturer's instructions.

Bake on a regular/white cycle.

Tarragon Bread

Buttermilk makes for a nice, tangy flavor but you can replace it either with plain milk or milk to which you've added 1 teaspoon of lemon juice or vinegar. Farmer's cheese may also be replaced by cottage cheese or ricotta.

7/8 c + 2 T buttermilk

2 t butter or margarine

2 c bread flour

1 t salt

2 t dried tarragon

4 oz. farmer's cheese, crumbled

2 t sugar

2 t yeast

Add the ingredients to your machine according to the manufacturer's instructions.

Bake on a regular or rapid cycle.

Hot Stuff Cajun Bread (Dairy-Free)

This is a fun, flavorful bread, perfect with Chile or Jambalaya!

3/4 c water

1 T butter or margarine

1/2 c chopped onion

1/2 c chopped green pepper

1 T sugar

2 t Cajun or Creole
  seasoned salt

1 t red pepper flakes

1/4 t Cayenne pepper

3 cloves garlic, minced

2 c bread flour

2 t yeast

Add the ingredients to your machine according to the manufacturer's instructions.

Bake on a regular, light, rapid or "super rapid" cycle.

This bread can be made on a timed cycle.

Toasted Sesame Bread (Dairy-Free)

This makes a very dense, tasty loaf.

Toast the sesame seeds by placing them in one layer on a cookie sheet and baking at 350 degrees for about 7 minutes.

1-1/4 c water	2 t salt
3 T olive oil	1 T sugar
2 c bread flour	1/3 c toasted sesame seeds
1 c whole wheat flour	2 t yeast
3 T wheat germ	

Add the ingredients to your machine according to the manufacturer's instructions.

Bake on a regular, light, or rapid cycle.

This recipe may be prepared on a timed cycle.

Wisconsin Dairyland Bread

There's lots of calcium in this delicious bread—and I told myself that over and over as I scarfed it down during my second pregnancy!

I like to use Nature's Seasoning mix for this, but you can use any seasoned salt, or a half a teaspoon of your favorite herb with and half teaspoon of salt.

3/4 c milk	2 c bread flour
1 c cottage cheese	1/2 t salt
1/2 c shredded sharp Wisconsin cheddar cheese	1/2 t seasoned salt
	2 t sugar
1 t butter or margarine	2–3 t yeast

Add the ingredients to your machine according to the manufacturer's instructions.

Bake on a regular, light, or rapid cycle

Light Wheat Ricotta Bread

This makes a nice, easily sliced, sandwich bread.

1 c ricotta cheese	1-1/2 c + 1 T bread flour
3/4 c milk	1 t salt
1 T butter or margarine	1 T sugar
3/4 c whole wheat flour	2–3 t yeast

Add the ingredients to your machine according to the manufacturer's instructions.

Bake on a regular/white, wheat, light, or rapid cycle.

Italian Spice Bread (Dairy-Free)

This is terrific with soups and stews.
The scent, as it bakes, it divine.

7/8 c water	2 t dried oregano
2 c bread flour	2 t dried marjoram
2 t sugar	1/4 t ground rosemary
1 t salt	4 cloves garlic, minced
2 t dried basil	2–3 t yeast

Add the ingredients to your machine according to the manufacturer's instructions.

Bake on a regular, light, or rapid cycle.

You may also prepare this bread on a timed cycle.

Rosemary Onion Bread (Dairy-Free)

A sophisticated bread for cold cut or cheese sandwiches!

3/4 c water

1/2 onion, finely chopped

2 c bread flour

2 t sugar

1 t salt

2 t dried rosemary

2 t yeast

Add the ingredients to your machine according to the manufacturer's instructions.

Bake on a regular, light, medium or rapid cycle.

This recipe may be prepared on a timed cycle.

Finnish Easter Bread

*This is an old recipe from my grandmother's collection, which
I've modified. I can't actually vouch for it as an authentic
Finnish Easter bread, but that would certainly
be a fine time to serve it!*

2/3 c milk

1/4 c light vegetable oil

1 egg yolk (save white)

1 t salt

1 t grated orange rind

1 t grated lemon rind

2 t mace

2 T white granulated sugar

2 c bread flour

2 t yeast

1/4 c currants

1/3 c sliced almonds

1 egg white (from above),
   whipped slightly with a fork
   or whisk

Add the ingredients to your machine, except the raisins, almonds, and
egg white, according to the manufacturer's instructions. Add the
raisins, almonds, and egg white at the indicator beep.

Bake on a sweet, regular/white, or rapid cycle. Serve warm with
Cream Cheese Spread (on next page).

CREAM CHEESE SPREAD

1 pkg (8 oz.) cream cheese,
  softened

1–2 T milk

1/2 tsp vanilla

pinch salt

2 c powdered sugar

In a small bowl, using a hand mixer, blend the cream cheese, milk, vanilla and salt to make a smooth consistency. Gradually add the powdered sugar and whip to a light consistency.

Greek Easter Bread

*The sweetness of this bread is quite subtle. It's nice with
either sweet butter, or a sweet cream cheese spread.*

2/3 c milk	1 t salt
3 T oil	1/4 c sugar
1 egg	2 c bread flour
1 t almond extract	2 t yeast
1 t vanilla extract	1/4 c slivered almonds

Add the ingredients to your machine, except the almonds, according to
the manufacturer's instructions. Add the almonds at the indicator beep.
Bake on a sweet, regular/white, or rapid cycle.

Peanut Butter Cap'n Crunch Bread

This is not the same as Crunchy Peanut Butter bread—once cooked,
the cereal in this bread no longer crunches, although it adds
a wonderful nutty flavor. This loaf is surprisingly
nice just toasted and buttered, but of course it's a big hit
for peanut butter and jelly sandwiches.

1 c milk	1 t salt
1 egg	2 T sugar
1 t butter or margarine	2 t yeast
1-3/4 + 3 T bread flour	
2 c peanut butter crunch breakfast cereal	

Add the ingredients to your machine according to the manufacturer's
instructions.

Bake on a regular/white, light, or rapid cycle

Banana Pecan Bread (Dairy-Free)

*If you don't like pecans, you may substitute walnuts.
As with all banana bread recipes, take a peek at the dough while
it's kneading, to make sure it's the right consistency. The
liquid content will vary here, according to how much banana you
use and how ripe they are, so you might need to add either
a touch more flour, or a touch of water. However, the dough
will be a little stickier than most, so don't look
for the usual smooth, elastic surface.*

1/2 c water	1/2 t salt
2 small ripe bananas	2 c + 1 T bread flour
1 T light vegetable oil	2 t yeast
2 t lemon juice	1/4 c chopped pecans
3 T white granulated sugar	

Add the ingredients to your machine, except the pecans, according to
the manufacturer's instructions. Add the pecans at the indicator beep.

Bake on a light or rapid cycle.

This recipe may be prepared on a timed cycle.

Blueberry Muffin Bread

*During my second pregnancy, when I was very ill, I ate this bread
(adapted from my favorite muffin recipe) almost exclusively
because it was the only thing my fussy tastes could tolerate! It
was pretty good nutrition in a very tasty package.*

*I use frozen blueberries usually, which works great but tends to make
the liquid to dry proportions a little tricky. If you're using
fresh blueberries, reduce the bread flour by 1/4–1/2 cup and
add flour by the tablespoonful, if necessary, to make
a slightly sticky loaf.*

3/4 c milk	2 T wheat germ
1 egg	1/4 c brown sugar
4 t butter or margarine	1 t salt
1/4 c sour cream	3 t yeast
2-1/2 c bread flour	1 c blueberries
2 c old fashioned rolled oats	

Add the ingredients to your machine, except the blueberries, according
to the manufacturer's instructions. Add the blueberries at the indicator
beep.

Bake on a regular/white, light, or rapid cycle.

Nutella Bread (Dairy-Free)

*Nutella spread not only gives this bread a delicious nutty
flavor, but it makes a terrific topping for the same.*

1 c water

1/2 c Nutella spread

1/2 t almond extract

2 c bread flour

1 t salt

1/2 c granulated sugar

1/4 c light brown sugar,
packed

2 t yeast

Add the ingredients to your machine according to the manufacturer's
instructions.

Bake on a regular, light, or rapid cycle

This can also be prepared on a timed cycle.

Mocha Cream Bread

This loaf doesn't rise quite as high as some others, but it's still light and spongy, with a delicious rich chocolate flavor. You may increase the coffee for more intensity, and use decaf if caffeine is a concern.

1/2 c heavy cream	1/4 c sugar
1/4 c + 3 T half and half	1 T brown sugar
2 eggs	1/3 c cocoa powder
3 T butter or margarine	1 t instant coffee crystals
2 c bread flour, divided	2 t yeast
1/2 t salt	

Put the cream into a saucepan and bring it to a light boil. Immediately add 1/2 cup of the bread flour and remove the pan from the heat. Stir rapidly to make a thick, mashed potato consistency and set aside to cool.

Add the remaining ingredients to the bread pan in the order suggested by your machine's manufacturer. Push start and add the cream and flour mixture.

This may be baked on a regular, light, or rapid cycle.

Traditional Jewish Challah

*This is my favorite white bread, perfect for everything
from toast to sandwiches to French Toast. I tend to leave the poppy
seeds out when I'm making it for the kids.*

1/2 c water	2 c bread flour
1 egg	1 t salt
1 egg yolk (save the white)	1 T sugar
5 t unsalted butter or	1 t poppy seeds, optional
margarine	2 t yeast

Stir 1 T milk into the egg white in a small bowl and set it aside.

Add the ingredients to your machine according to the manufacturer's instructions.

After the final knead, paint the egg white mixture on top of the loaf to make a shiny glaze.

Bake on a French, regular/white, light, or rapid cycle.

Light Raspberry Bread

This is a very tangy, high-rising bread.

*When you add the yogurt to the machine, you might want
to save the fruit from the bottom and add it at the
indicator beep, to keep the fruit more intact.*

1/4 c skim milk	1 T butter or margarine
1 c raspberry yogurt	1/2 t salt
3 T frozen raspberries	2 c bread flour
1 T honey	2 t yeast

Add the ingredients to your machine according to the manufacturer's
instructions.

Bake on a regular/white, light, or rapid cycle.

Raisin Bran Bread

*This is another fun cereal bread, easy
to make and easy to eat.*

1 c milk	1 t salt
2 T butter or margarine	2 T brown sugar
2 c bread flour	2 T granulated sugar
1 c raisin bran cereal	2–3 t yeast

Add the ingredients to your machine according to the manufacturer's instructions.

Bake on a regular/white, light, or rapid cycle.

Summer Breads

Summer's bounty includes sweet basil, ripe red

tomatoes, sweet bell peppers, vidalia onions,

and delicious tender zucchini. So do the

breads in this summer section. Look here

for the perfect accompaniment to your

patio cookout or dinner

on the porch.

Grandma's Home-Baked White Bread

*This is the classic white bread, good for everything
from toast to sandwiches.*

3/4 c + 1 T milk	2 t sugar
2 T butter or margarine	1 t salt
2 c bread flour	2–3 t yeast

Add the ingredients to your machine according to the manufacturer's instructions.

Bake on a regular/white, light, or rapid cycle.

Rosemary–Olive Wheat Bread

*If you're looking for the perfect bread to take to a
cook-out pot luck, look no further!*

2/3 c water	1/3 c whole wheat flour
1/3 c milk	1/2 c pitted Spanish olives
4 t olive oil	5 T cornmeal
1 T sugar	1/3 c minced onion
1/4 t salt	1 t dried rosemary
1/4 t freshly ground pepper	3 t yeast
1-2/3 c bread flour	

Add the ingredients to your machine according to the manufacturer's
instructions.

Bake on a regular/wheat, white, light, or rapid cycle.

Basil Parmesan Bread

*The cottage cheese adds a delicate moisture to this loaf, and
you can use regular or low-fat. Serve thin slices of this bread with
pesto spread and lots of glasses of red wine!*

1/2 c + 3 T c milk

1 c cottage cheese

1/2 c shredded Parmesan cheese
or pecorino Romano cheese

2 c bread flour

3/4 t salt

1/2 t freshly ground black
pepper (or more, to taste)

3 T fresh, or 2 t dried, basil

1 T sugar

2 t olive oil

2–3 t yeast

Add the ingredients to your machine according to the manufacturer's
instructions.

Bake on a regular/white, light, or rapid cycle.

Cornmeal Herb Bread

*Cornmeal can certainly make a nice difference in a bread,
particularly this one. It produces a delicate crunch
on the outside with a lovely tender inside.*

*You can pick and choose your favorite herbs, you needn't
follow my guidelines. Just one word of caution: be careful not to
be too heavy-handed with dried herbs as they tend to
impart a very strong flavor.*

1 c evaporated milk	1 t salt
1/3 c water	1/2 t celery seed
2 t butter or margarine	3/4 t dried sage
2 c bread flour	1/2 t dried rosemary
1/4 c cornmeal	1/4 t dried marjoram
4 t light brown sugar	2 t yeast

Add the ingredients to your machine according to the manufacturer's instructions.

Bake on a regular/white, light, or rapid cycle.

Secret Ingredient Chocolate Bread

*I love this recipe! The pepper is the secret ingredient,
giving the cocoa a bit of crackle.*

1 c + 2 T half-and-half, scalded	1/2 c brown sugar
2 eggs	1 T white sugar
1-1/2 c bread flour	1/2 t salt
3/4 c whole wheat flour	3/4 t freshly ground pepper
1 c rolled oats	1/2 c cocoa powder
	3 t yeast

Add the ingredients to your machine according to the manufacturer's
instructions.

Bake on a regular/white, light, or rapid cycle.

This recipe may be prepared on a timed cycle.

Sally Lunn Bread

*The story is that Sally Lunn was a little girl who sold
these special, tasty bread buns on a street corner in Europe.
I have no idea if it's true, but the bread sure is good.*

1/2 c + 2 T milk	1 t salt
2 large eggs	2 T sugar
4 T butter or margarine	2–3 t yeast
2 c bread flour	

Add the ingredients to your machine according to the manufacturer's instructions.

Bake on a regular/white, light, or rapid cycle.

Tuscan Rosemary Bread (Dairy-Free)

This recipe, with its profusion of fresh rosemary, is impossible to imitate exactly with dried rosemary. However, you can make a nice loaf, if not exactly the same, by substituting 2 t dried rosemary for the fresh.

7/8 c water

1 t honey

2 c bread flour

2 t cornmeal

1/4 c chopped fresh rosemary

1 t salt

1/2 t ground black pepper

1 clove garlic, minced

2–3 t yeast

Add the ingredients to your machine according to the manufacturer's instructions.

Bake on a regular/white, light, or rapid cycle.

Bagel Bread (Dairy-Free)

This is a new favorite of mine! Absolutely delicious!

I like to add Omega-3 rich flaxseed instead of, or in addition to, the poppy and sesame seeds.

1 c water

1 T light vegetable oil

3 T minced onion, sauteed in butter or margarine and cooled

2 cups bread flour

1 T sugar

1 t salt

1 t sesame seeds

1 t poppy seeds

2 t yeast

Add the ingredients to your machine according to the manufacturer's instructions.

Bake on a regular/white, light, or rapid cycle.

Savory Italian Dinner Bread

*I make this often in the summer and enjoy topping it with
Vidalia onion slices, and a bit of Romano cheese, then broiling it for just
a few minutes before serving with a nice spread of pesto.*

3/4 c + 2 T water

1 T olive oil

1/4 c grated pecorino
   Romano cheese

1/4 c grated Parmesan cheese

1 t salt

2 t sugar

3 T chopped fresh basil, or
   2 t dried basil

2 c bread flour

2–3 t yeast

Add the ingredients to your machine according to the manufacturer's
instructions.

Use a regular/white, light, or rapid bread cycle.

Cashew Gouda Cheese Bread

*You may prefer to use the slightly sharper Edam cheese for
this bread, but I prefer the buttery smoothness of
Gouda with the cashew nuts.*

1 c milk	1 t salt
2 t butter or margarine	1/4 c cashew pieces
2 c bread flour	1/4 c shredded Gouda cheese
2 t sugar	2 t yeast

Add the ingredients to your machine according to the manufacturer's
instructions.

Use a regular/white, light, or rapid bread cycle.

Provençal Garlic Bread (Dairy-Free)

Normally I try to use fresh garlic whenever possible, but for this bread I use minced garlic from a jar. It's easier to measure and in the final product I think the flavor is comparable to what you'd get with fresh garlic.

7/8 c water

1 T olive oil

1 T minced garlic (about 3–4 cloves)

1/4 c chopped red pepper

1 T sugar

1 t salt

2 c bread flour

1 t herbes de Provence

2 t yeast

Add the ingredients to your machine according to the manufacturer's instructions.

Bake on a regular/white, light, or rapid cycle.

This bread may also be prepared on a timed cycle.

Greek Feta Bread

*I use a mild feta for this particular bread. Feta, particularly
sharp feta, is a salty cheese, so I don't like to
add any additional salt.*

7/8 c buttermilk	2 c bread flour
1 egg	2 t sugar
3–4 T crumbled feta cheese	2 t yeast

Add the ingredients to your machine according to the manufacturer's
instructions.

Bake on a regular/white, light, or rapid cycle.

Peppery Garlic Bread

*If you don't like the zest of black pepper and fresh
garlic, I suggest you skip this loaf altogether. I like the pepper very
coarsely ground, but you may use finely ground pepper
for a more subtle flavor.*

1 c water

2 t sugar

3/4 t salt

3 cloves fresh garlic, minced

1-1/2 t coarsely ground black
  pepper

2 c bread flour

1/4 c Parmesan or Romano
  cheese

2 t yeast

Add the ingredients to your machine according to the manufacturer's
instructions.

Bake on a regular/white, light, or rapid cycle.

Sun-Dried Tomato Pizza Bread

*You may sprinkle grated cheese (mozzarella, cheddar, or whatever
your favorite is) on this bread ten minutes before the end of
the baking cycle. Don't worry about cleaning the machine afterwards—
when the cheese is cooled, you just peel it off.*

*Check the dough after it's been kneading for about 15–20 minutes.
Sometimes the reconstituted tomatoes hold a lot of water, and
you might need to add a couple of tablespoons of flour.*

1 c tomato juice, V-8, or water	1/2 t salt
1 T olive oil	2 T sugar
1 T butter or margarine	3/4 t dried oregano
1/2 c pecorino Romano or Parmesan cheese	2 t yeast
1/2 c mozzarella or "pizza mix" cheese	1/2 c sun-dried tomatoes, reconstituted in water, then drained
2 c bread flour	

Add the ingredients to your machine, except the sun-dried tomatoes,
according to the manufacturer's instructions. Add the tomatoes at the
indicator beep.

Bake on a regular/white, light, or rapid cycle.

Ranch Bread

*This is a sticky dough and ends up as a rather heavy loaf, which tastes
like unbelievably rich, creamy dinner rolls. Your guests will be surprised
that the "secret ingredient" is ranch dressing, since the flavor is so subtle.*

Delicious with a meatloaf or Salisbury steak dinner!

3/4 c buttermilk	3 T sugar
2 T milk	1/2 t salt
2 c bread flour	2–3 t yeast
1 (1 oz) package of ranch dressing mix	

Add the ingredients to your machine according to the manufacturer's
instructions.

Bake on a regular/white, light, or rapid cycle.

Sun–Dried Tomato Polenta Bread (Dairy-Free)

*Use dried sun-dried tomatoes, reconstituted in boiling water
and well drained for this recipe. I like to simply cut them into thirds
with kitchen shears, but you may chop them as finely or coarsely as you
like. If the only sun-dried tomatoes you can find are already in
oil, drain them well, omit the olive oil and 1 tablespoon of water
from this recipe, then peek at the dough as it's kneading to make
sure it's smooth and elastic. If it's too loose or looks like batter, add flour
by the tablespoon until it reaches the right consistency.*

3/4 c + 1 T water	1 t dried basil
2 t olive oil	2 cloves garlic, finely chopped
2 c bread flour	3 t yeast
1/4 c cornmeal	1/4 c sun-dried tomatoes,
1 t salt	chopped
1 t sugar	1/4 c minced onion

Add the ingredients to your machine according to the manufacturer's
instructions.

Bake on a regular/white, light, or rapid cycle.

This recipe may also be prepared using a timed cycle.

Honey Feta Bread

A little feta goes a long way in this flavorful loaf!
Very nice with a Greek salad for dinner.

2/3 c + 1 T water

1 egg

1 T honey

2 c bread flour

1 t salt

4 oz. feta cheese

2 t yeast

Add the ingredients to your machine according to the manufacturer's instructions.

Bake on a regular/white, light, or rapid cycle.

Milk and Honey Bread

This is a very nice recipe for childrens' sandwich bread,
but because of the honey I wouldn't serve it to a child under 2.

2/3 c milk

2 T honey

1 egg

2 T butter or margarine

2/3 c old-fashioned rolled oats

2 c bread flour

3/4 t salt

2 t yeast

Add the ingredients to your machine according to the manufacturer's instructions.

Bake on a regular/white, light, or rapid cycle.

"Smells Sooooo Good"
Gruyère Cheese Bread

*This is one of the nicest, most moist cheese breads I've made,
and I love it just plain, hot out of the machine.*

*The quality of the cheese is important when you're talking Gruyère.
Always go for the best imported Gruyère you can buy. If you're
feeling really extravagant, use this as the bread for French
Onion Soup, also topped with good Gruyère.*

1/2 c milk

1/3 c water

1 egg

2 t butter or margarine

1 t salt

1 T + 1 t sugar

2-1/4 c bread flour

2/3 c grated Gruyère (or
   1 c small cubes, to be added
   at indicator beep)

2 t yeast

Add the ingredients to your machine, except for the cheese chunks, in
the order suggested by the manufacturer. Add the cheese chunks when
the indicator beeps.

Bake on a regular/white, light, or rapid cycle.

Banana Oat Bran Bread (Dairy-Free)

This makes a short, dense loaf. It's not very banana-y when it's done, so it's really nice with butter and jam.

As with other banana recipes, the water content here depends on how ripe the bananas are. Begin by adding 3/4 cup, and add a tablespoon at a time as necessary, if necessary.

3/4 c water	2 t nutmeg
1 large ripe banana	1-3/4 c bread flour
4 t molasses	3/4 c whole wheat flour
2 T apple jelly	3/4 c oat bran
1 t salt	2 t yeast

Add the ingredients to your machine according to the manufacturer's instructions.

Bake on a sweet, regular/white, light, or rapid cycle.

Crunchy Peanut Butter and Honey Bread (Dairy-Free)

*I make this one for the taste and texture, but an added bonus
is that it has some protein in it. This is particularly
good on those days when my husband is in too big a
hurry to have a nutritious breakfast.*

*The final product looks very pretty when topped
with oats after the final knead.*

1 c water

1 t honey

1/3 c crunchy peanut butter

2 c bread flour

1/4 c quick oats

1/2 t salt

3 T brown sugar

2 t yeast

1/4 c dry roasted peanuts

Add all the ingredients to your machine, except the peanuts, according to the manufacturer's instructions. Add the peanuts at the indicator beep.

Bake on a sweet, regular/white, light, or rapid cycle.

You may also prepare this bread on a timed cycle.

Sweet Tropical Bread

*What a terrific recipe this is! Moist and slightly sweet,
it is the perfect breakfast bread.*

*The only trick is that you must keep an eye on the dough while it's
kneading, because the banana and pineapple add unpredictable
amounts of liquid to the dough. If it looks too much like batter,
add 1 tablespoon of bread flour at a time until you have a
smooth, elastic loaf.*

3 T milk

1 egg

1/3 c canned pineapple
chunks, drained

2 T pineapple juice (from
drained chunks, above)

1 small banana

2 c + 2 T bread flour

1/4 c whole wheat flour

1/4 c chopped macadamia
nuts

1/3 c shredded coconut,
toasted to light brown

2 T butter or margarine

1 T granulated sugar

1 T brown sugar

1 t salt

1/4 t baking soda

2 t yeast

Add all the ingredients to your machine according to the manufacturer's
instructions (or, if you'd like the macadamia nuts to remain more
intact, add them when the indicator beeps).

Bake on a sweet, regular/white, light, or rapid cycle.

Zucchini Bisque n' Bread

This soup is such a stunner that I tried all kinds of breads to see which one was "perfect" to serve with it. Then one day I tried making a bread out of the soup itself. It took a couple of tries but eventually I ended up with a beautiful loaf that tasted divine when spread with butter and served with the soup. At the moment, it is my favorite.

1 c zucchini bisque (recipe on next page)
1/2 t salt, optional (depending on how much salt you put in the soup)

2 c bread flour
1 T sugar
2 t yeast

Add the ingredients to your machine according to the manufacturer's instructions.

Bake on a white or medium bread cycle.

ZUCCHINI BISQUE

This recipe is completely forgiving. You can use heavy cream, half-and-half, or milk, you can use more or less butter, and you can use just about any vegetable and certainly any squash. You may also serve it hot or cold. Everyone will love it.

2 lbs. zucchini or other
   squash, peeled and chopped
1 large onion, peeled and
   chopped
4 T butter or margarine
3 c chicken stock
1 t dried basil
1/2 t ground nutmeg
salt and pepper, to taste

1 c whole milk or half-and-
   half (skim works, but is not
   as good)
1/2 cup mashed potato flakes,
   approximately (depending
   on how thick you want
   the bisque)

Heat the butter or margarine in a large pan, and add the onions. Cook until they're translucent.

Add the zucchini and 1/2 cup of the chicken stock. Sauté for 10 minutes, then add all of the ingredients except the milk or half-and-half. Cook until the squash is tender, then purée the soup until smooth (an immersion blender is great for this).

Add the milk and mashed potato flakes, heat through, and taste to see if you need to adjust the seasoning. Serve.

Applesauce Yogurt Bread

This is a nice tangy fruit bread, with a terrific crumb.

1/2 c plain or vanilla yogurt	1 T sugar
1/2 c applesauce	1/2 t salt
1/4 c half-and-half (or milk)	2 T butter or margarine
2 c bread flour	2 t yeast

Add the ingredients to your machine according to the manufacturer's instructions.

Bake on a sweet, regular/white, light, or rapid cycle.

Banana Wheat Bread

This is a tricky bread since, because of the high amount of honey and sugars from the fruit, it burns easily. I recommend checking it during the last ten minutes of baking, no matter which cycle you use, in order to prevent it from burning. For that reason, this isn't a good candidate for a timed cycle.

The dough will be very sticky and soft—resist the urge to add too much flour, or you'll end up with a powdery taste. Also, the riper the bananas, the more banana flavor the bread will have.

1/3 c applesauce	1-1/2 c + 2 T bread flour
1/3 c honey	1 c whole wheat flour
1 egg	1 t salt
1 t vanilla	2–3 t yeast
2 medium bananas, the riper the better	

Add the ingredients to your machine according to the manufacturer's instructions.

Bake on a sweet, regular/white, regular/wheat, light or rapid cycle.

Macadamia Banana Bread (Dairy-Free)

This is a major favorite around my house! It's not as sweet as you might expect (though a lot of that has to do with how ripe the bananas are—the riper they are, the sweeter the bread is), but it can really be dressed up with some cinnamon sugar and butter.

If the macadamia nuts you use are salted, try to brush them off just a little bit, and omit the salt from the other ingredients.

1/2 c water	1/2 t salt
2 small ripe bananas	2 c + 1 T bread flour
1 T butter or margarine	2 t yeast
2 t lemon juice	1/4 c macadamia nuts
3 T brown sugar	

Add the ingredients to your machine, except the macadamia nuts, according to the manufacturer's instructions.

Bake on a sweet, regular/white, light or rapid cycle.

This recipe may be prepared on a timed cycle.

Strawberry Yogurt Bread

As with other yogurt breads, you may use a "light" yogurt for this bread, but try to avoid fat-free yogurt that may contain aspartame.

This is terrific for peanut butter and jelly sandwiches!

3/4 c strawberry yogurt	2 c bread flour
1/4 c milk	1/2 t salt
1 egg	2 T butter or margarine
1 T honey	2 t yeast
1 T strawberry jam	

Add the ingredients to your machine according to the manufacturer's instructions.

Bake on a sweet, regular/white, light, or rapid cycle.

Apple Walnut Bread (Dairy-Free)

This is the ultimate cinnamon toast bread! I like to use sweet apples,
like Gala or Fuji, and add the chunks at the indicator beep.

3/4 c apple juice	2 T brown sugar
1 T butter or margarine	2 t granulated sugar
1-3/4 c bread flour	1/4 c raisins, optional
1 c old-fashioned rolled oats	1 small apple, cored, peeled
2 T oat bran	and chopped (about 1/2 c)
1 t salt	1/4 c chopped walnuts
1-1/2 t cinnamon	3 scant t yeast

Add the ingredients to your machine, except the raisins and walnuts
(and apple pieces, if you choose), according to the manufacturer's
instructions.

Add the raisins and walnuts at the indicator beep or up to 5 minutes
before the end of the final knead. Alternatively, you may choose to add
everything at the beginning and let it be kneaded smoothly into the
bread.

Bake on a sweet, regular/white, light, or rapid cycle.

Lemon Poppyseed Bread

The acidity of the lemon juice gives this loaf a lovely light texture, making it perfect for tea on a summer afternoon. If you use fresh, homemade lemonade—as opposed to frozen or already prepared—you might want to reduce the lemon extract by half, or leave it out altogether.

3/4 c lemonade	3 T sugar
2 T water	1 t lemon zest
1/2 t lemon extract	2 t poppyseeds
1 egg	2 c bread flour
2 t butter or margarine	2 t yeast
3/4 t salt	

Add the ingredients to your machine according to the manufacturer's instructions.

Bake on a sweet, regular/white, light, or rapid cycle.

You may also prepare this bread on a timed cycle.

Pecan Peach Bread

A real Georgia treat!

Peaches come with varying amounts of moisture, so you have to watch this dough a little in the beginning of the kneading cycle. If it looks too dry, add water to make a smooth elastic consistency.

This makes a dense, moist loaf.

2 T buttermilk, or milk to
   which you've added 1
   teaspoon of lemon juice
   or vinegar
1 t almond extract
1 c bread flour
1/2 c whole wheat flour
1 t salt
4 t butter or margarine,
   softened or melted

4 t sugar
4 t brown sugar
1 c peeled and chopped fresh
   peaches, drained
water, if necessary
2 t yeast
1/4 c pecan pieces

Add all the ingredients to your machine, except the pecans, according to the manufacturer's instructions. Add the pecans at the indicator beep.

Bake on a sweet, regular/white, light, or rapid cycle.

You may also prepare this bread on a timed cycle.

Autumn Breads

When the days grow shorter and the holidays
are coming, it's time to take advantage of the
fall harvest. In this section you'll find spicy
pumpkin breads, tart cranberry breads, sweet
apple and pear loaves, as well as sweet cinnamon
loaves, dessert cocoa breads, and the perfect
rye for leftover turkey sandwiches.

Cheddar Dill Bread

*One of my husband's all-time favorite snacks is super-sharp cheddar
cheese and crackers with sliced dill pickles on the side. I never understood
the full appeal of this combination until I tried it myself. Once
I did, I immediately set about inventing a bread that combined
those same two tastes, although milder. Here it is!*

1 c + 1 T whole buttermilk	1/4 t salt
1 egg	1 T sugar
1-1/2 c bread flour	2 t yeast
2/3 c pastry flour	1 c of 1/2-inch cheddar cheese
1 t dried dill weed	chunks

Add all the ingredients to your machine, except the cheese chunks,
according to the manufacturer's instructions. Add the cheese at the
indicator beep.

Bake on a regular/white or light cycle.

Irish Stout Bread

This hearty bread makes a good cold cuts sandwich.

1/2 c water

1/2 c warm stout ale (such as
  Guinness or Whitneys)

1/4 c maple syrup

2 c bread flour

1/2 c whole wheat flour

1 c instant plain oatmeal

1/2 c cornmeal

1-1/2 t salt

2 egg whites

3 t yeast

Add the ingredients to your machine according to the manufacturer's instructions.

Bake on a regular/white or regular/wheat cycle.

French Country Bread

*This is a classic—perfect to hollow out and
make bread bowls for soup!*

3/4 c water	1 t salt
2 egg whites, stiffly beaten	1 T sugar
4 t butter or margarine	2–3 t yeast
2 c bread flour	

Add the ingredients to your machine according to the manufacturer's instructions.

Bake on a French, regular, light, or rapid cycle.

This bread may be prepared on a timed cycle.

Double Cheese Wheat Bread

This is a lovely moist cheese bread with a mild flavor.

1 c ricotta cheese

3/4 c milk

1 t butter or margarine

1/2 c shredded sharp cheddar
  cheese

3/4 c whole wheat flour

1-1/2 c + 1 T bread flour

1/2 t salt

2 t sugar

2–3 t yeast

Add the ingredients to your machine according to the manufacturer's instructions.

Bake on a regular/white, regular/wheat, light, or rapid cycle.

Tex-Mex Spicy
Beer n' Cheese Bread

You may choose to shred all the cheese, and add them all at
the beginning, for convenience, and for one, smoothly cheesy loaf
(if you use already-seasoned cheese, omit the chili powder
from this recipe). If you add the cheese later, cut into 1/4-inch cubes,
you'll have a chunkier cheese bread.

I like to use Mexican beer, such as Corona, for this recipe.

1 c beer	2 c bread flour
1 T butter or margarine	1 t chili powder
4 oz. sharp cheddar cheese	1 T sugar
3 oz Monterey Jack cheese	1 t salt
1–2 t chopped jalapeños	2 t yeast
3 T mild green chilies	

Add the ingredients to your machine, except for the jalapeños (and the cheese, if you want it chunkier), according to the manufacturer's instructions.

At the indicator, add the jalapeño and any cheese you may have divided.

Use a regular/white or rapid bread cycle.

This bread can be prepared on a timed cycle, up to six hours in advance (don't worry about adding the peppers and cheeses in advance —the texture of the loaf will be slightly different, but the taste is still wonderful).

New England Anadama Bread (Dairy-Free)

Anadama is a classic New England grain bread.

1 c water	1/4 c corn meal
1 T butter or margarine	1 t salt
3 T molasses	2–3 t yeast
2 c bread flour	

Add the ingredients to your machine according to the manufacturer's instructions.

Bake on a regular/white, light, or rapid cycle.

This bread may be prepared on a timed cycle.

Fruit and Cereal Bread

You can use Muesli or Post "Fruit & Fibre" for this bread, which has some of the benefits of whole grains, because of the cereal, but maintains a fine, tender texture. It's terrific for breakfast.

1c buttermilk	2 T brown sugar
2 T light vegetable oil	1/2 t salt
2 c bread flour	2 t yeast
1 c cereal	

Add the ingredients to your machine according to the manufacturer's instructions.

Bake on a regular/white, light, or rapid cycle.

This bread may be prepared on a timed cycle.

Cream and Cheese Bread

*You may use regular Swiss or even light
Swiss Cheese for this recipe.*

*If you like to have gooey chunks of cheese in your cheese bread,
rather than a uniform cheese flavor, add the cheese
in 1/4-inch chunks at the indicator beep.*

1/3 c water	2 c shredded Swiss cheese
1/4 c buttermilk	2 c + 2 T bread flour
1/4 c heavy cream	1 t salt
1 egg	1 T sugar
1 T butter or margarine	2 t yeast

Add the ingredients to your machine according to the manufacturer's instructions.

Bake on a regular/white, light, or rapid cycle.

Whole Wheat Sour Cream Bread

This is a variation on one of my favorites, Sour Cream Bread. It makes a nice, light wheat bread, good for toast or sandwiches.

1/4 c sour cream (light or regular)	1-1/4 c bread flour
2/3 c half-and-half	3/4 c whole wheat flour
1/4 c + 1 T milk	1 t salt
1 T honey	1 t baking soda
	2 t yeast

Add the ingredients to your machine according to the manufacturer's instructions.

Bake on a regular/wheat, regular/white, or rapid cycle.

Chips n' Beer Bread (Dairy-Free)

*Looking for the perfect bread to eat during
football games? Look no further!*

*This is particularly nice with cheese spread, or for grilled cheese
sandwiches, even for hamburgers. Personally, I like to use flavored
Doritos, but you can use whatever chips you like best.*

1 c flat beer

1 t vegetable oil

2 c bread flour

1/2 c finely crumbled tortilla
  chips (flavored or not)

2 t sugar

2–3 t yeast

Add the ingredients to your machine according to the manufacturer's
instructions.

Use a regular/white or rapid bread cycle.

This bread can be prepared on a timed cycle.

Triple Whammy Buttermilk Gorgonzola and Cheddar Bread

This is a fine textured bread, and extremely easy to slice.

I've used Gorgonzola, Stilton, and generic blue cheese with this recipe, all with excellent results. Limburger works as well. The cheddar I usually have on hand is Cracker Barrel Extra Sharp, but if you prefer a milder cheddar, you can use one.

1 c buttermilk

1 T butter or margarine

1 egg

1/3 c grated cheddar cheese

3 T crumbled Gorgonzola
   Dolce or other blue cheese

1/2 t salt

1/2 c oatmeal

2 c + 3 T bread flour

2 t yeast

Add the ingredients to your machine according to the manufacturer's instructions.

Use a regular/white, light, or rapid bread cycle.

Instant Potato Bread

Here's a quick, easy way to make potato bread.

1 c milk	1 t salt
4 t butter or margarine	1 T sugar
2 c + 1 T bread flour	2–3 t yeast
1/4 c instant mashed	
potato flakes	

Add the ingredients to your machine according to the manufacturer's instructions.

Bake on a regular/white, light, or rapid cycle.

Farmer's Beer Bread

*I use a very mild domestic beer for this recipe, to allow the onions
to provide the highest note of flavor. Because they go
into the recipe raw, the smell of onions is quite pleasantly
strong while this loaf bakes.*

7/8 c warm, flat beer	2-1/2 c + 1 T bread flour
1/2 c chopped onion	1 T sugar
4 oz. farmer's cheese,	1 t salt
crumbled	2-3 t yeast

Add the ingredients to your machine according to the manufacturer's
instructions.

Use a regular, light, or rapid bread cycle.

Rye Crisps Cracker Loaf (Dairy-Free)

*At first I thought this bread was a flop because it didn't rise very
much. Then I took it out of the pan and sliced it and saw it had a
nice texture inside. So I made thin slices, then crisped them
in the oven and discovered they were just marvelous as "crackers"
for spreads and dips, especially with sharp cheeses.*

1 c water	1 t salt
1 T canola oil	1 t poppy seeds
1 t honey	1 t sesame seeds
1 T molasses	1 t caraway seeds
1-1/2 c bread flour	1 t fennel seeds
1/2 c rye flour	2 T pecan nuts
1/4 c buckwheat flour	3 t yeast
1 T cocoa powder	

Add the ingredients to your machine according to the manufacturer's
instructions.

Use a regular, light, or rapid bread cycle.

Walnut Bread

*I've experimented with many variation of the wonderful
blue cheese/walnut combination, and this
is one of my favorites.*

*There is a strange tendency for various buttermilks to have different
consistencies, so take a look at this while it's kneading—you might
actually find that you need to add a couple of teaspoons of
milk (plain or buttermilk will do fine) to make the
dough elastic enough.*

1 c buttermilk	1 t salt
1 t canola oil	1/4 c crumbled blue cheese
2 c bread flour	1/4 c walnut pieces
2 t sugar	2 t yeast

Add the ingredients to your machine according to the manufacturer's
instructions.

Use a regular/white, light, or rapid bread cycle.

Triple Cheese Bread

One of my favorite pizza parlors uses a combination of cheddar and Romano cheeses for its distinctive pizza, so I decided to try the same in bread. The cottage cheese is an added bonus to make the bread moist and tender.

I like to use Nature's Seasoning for this, but you can use any seasoned salt, or a half a teaspoon of your favorite herb with and half teaspoon of salt.

3/4 c milk	1/2 t salt
1 c cottage cheese	1/2 t seasoned salt
1/4 c shredded sharp cheddar cheese	2 t sugar
1/4 c Pecorino Romano	1 t butter or margarine
2 c bread flour	2–3 t yeast

Add the ingredients to your machine according to the manufacturer's instructions.

Bake on a regular/white, light, or rapid cycle.

English Muffin Bread

This is a longtime favorite!

7/8 c water	1 t salt
2 c bread flour	2 t sugar
1/4 t baking soda	2–3 t yeast
2 T nonfat dry milk powder	

Add the ingredients to your machine according to the manufacturer's instructions.

Bake on a regular, light, or rapid cycle.

Bran Chex Bread

This is a light, airy loaf, with a good crumb and tender inside . . . you'd never know it had healthy bran inside! Even my finicky ten year old loved it!

2/3 c milk	1 c Bran Chex Cereal
1/3 c water	1 t salt
2 t butter or margarine	1 T brown sugar
2 c bread flour	2 t yeast

Add the ingredients to your machine according to the manufacturer's instructions.

Bake on a regular/white, regular/wheat, light, or rapid cycle.

Sour Cream Onion and Dill Bread

A lovely combination! You may use low-fat versions of both the sour cream and the cottage cheese, if you prefer.

1/2 c sour cream	1/4 t baking soda
1/2 c cottage cheese	1 t salt
1/2 c + 1 T water	2 T minced dried onion
1 large egg	4 t dried dill weed
1 T butter or margarine	1 T sugar
2 c bread flour	2–3 t yeast

Add the ingredients to your machine according to the manufacturer's instructions.

Bake on a regular/white, light, or rapid cycle.

Tender Wheat Bread

*Don't be fooled by the seemingly dull proposition of
"wheat bread." This simple recipe yields a moist
loaf that's marvelous for sandwiches.*

3/4 c water	3/4 c whole wheat flour
1 egg	1 t salt
2 T light vegetable oil	3 T granulated sugar
1-1/2 c bread flour	2 t yeast

Add the ingredients to your machine according to the manufacturer's
instructions.

Bake on a regular/wheat, light, or rapid cycle.

Lora Brody's Challah

*I found this recipe in Lora Brody's wonderful cookbook,
PLUGGED IN. It's one of my all-time favorites for breakfast because
it's a tender bread with a wonderfully tender crumb, thanks
to the whole wheat pastry flour (which you can find at your local
grocery store). If you'd like to try braiding it into a traditional
challah bread braid, Lora makes a "dough relaxer" product
that keeps the dough from springing back into a ball when
you're trying to make shaped breads. E-mail Lora at
Blanche007@aol.com for a free sample.*

3/4 c water	1-1/2 t salt
2 extra large eggs	1 c whole wheat pastry flour
1/4 c vegetable oil	2 c all-purpose flour
3 T honey	2–3 t yeast

Add the ingredients to your machine according to the manufacturer's
instructions.

Bake on a regular, light, medium or rapid cycle.

Dark Pumpernickel (Dairy-Free)

This is tops for turkey sandwiches!

3/4 c water	2/3 c white flour
1 T vegetable oil	2/3 c whole wheat flour
3 T molasses	3/4 t salt
3 T Dutch processed cocoa	3 t caraway seeds, optional
powder	2–3 t yeast
2/3 c rye flour	

Add the ingredients to your machine according to the manufacturer's instructions.

Bake on a regular, light, or medium cycle.

This bread may be prepared on a timed cycle.

Buckwheat Potato Bread

This is an excellent choice for French Toast—it's a great way to get some whole grain nutrition into the kids without them realizing it.

3/4 c milk	3 T instant potato flakes
2 large eggs	1-1/2 c bread flour
2 T butter	1/4 c buckwheat flour
1 T honey	1/2 c whole wheat flour
1 t salt	2–3 t yeast

Add the ingredients to your machine according to the manufacturer's instructions.

Bake on a regular, light, medium or rapid cycle.

Cranberry Pumpkin Bread (Dairy-Free)

I like to use Craisins for this recipe, but if you like a more tart cranberry taste, you can reconstitute dried cranberries in boiling water, drain, and use them instead. If you like, you may use pumpkin pie filling instead of plain canned pumpkin, and omit the nutmeg, ginger, and cinnamon.

3/4 c water	1/4 t nutmeg
1 T light vegetable oil	1/4 t ginger
3 T brown sugar	1/2 t cinnamon
1/2 c canned pumpkin	3 t yeast
2 c + 2 T bread flour	1/4 c dried cranberries or
1 t salt	Craisins

Add the ingredients to your machine, except the cranberries, according to the manufacturer's instructions. Add the cranberries at the indicator beep.

Bake on a regular, light, or rapid cycle.

Sweet Crunch Cereal Bread

You may use any sweet crunch cereal for this recipe, brand name or generic, as long as it's a sweet kids' cereal and not a dense whole grain cereal. This is a lovely breakfast bread, for kids and adults!

1 c milk	2 c sweet crunch cereal
1 egg	1 t salt
1 t butter or margarine	2 T sugar
2 c bread flour	2 t yeast

Add the ingredients to your machine according to the manufacturer's instructions.

Bake on a regular, light, or rapid cycle

Applesauce Bread (Dairy-Free)

This is a crusty bread, with a tender middle and the delightful essence of apple. It makes wonderful cinnamon toast or French toast.

1 c applesauce	3 T sugar
2 T water	1 t cinnamon
1 T butter or margarine	1/8 t nutmeg
1-3/4 c bread flour	1/4 t allspice
1/2 c wheat bread	2–3 t yeast
1/2 t salt	

Add the ingredients to your machine according to the manufacturer's instructions.

Use a regular, light, or rapid bread cycle.

Spiced Cream Bread

This is lovely on chilly fall mornings.

3/4 c half-and-half	1/4 t allspice
3 T butter or margarine	1/4 t nutmeg
2 c bread flour	1/2 t salt
1 T sugar	2–3 t yeast
1 t cinnamon	

Add the ingredients to your machine according to the manufacturer's instructions.

Use a sweet, regular/white, light, or rapid bread cycle.

This bread can be prepared on a timed cycle.

Multi-Berry Yogurt Bread

Use the berries frozen for this recipe and add them at the indicator beep. They won't stay completely intact, but they'll come close.

1 c boysenberry yogurt	1 T honey
2 T milk	1/2 t salt
1/2 c frozen mixed berries	2 T butter or margarine
2 c bread flour	2 t yeast

Add the ingredients to your machine, except the frozen berries, according to the manufacturer's instructions.

Add the frozen berries three minutes *after* the indicator beep.

Bake on a regular, light, or rapid cycle.

Spiced Rum After Dinner Bread (Dairy-Free)

This is basically a sweet white bread with a little extra kick.

1/2 c water	1/2 t salt
1 T + 2 t spiced rum	1/4 c sugar
1 t light vegetable oil	2 c bread flour
1 t butter or margarine	2 t yeast

Add the ingredients to your machine according to the manufacturer's instructions.

Bake on a regular, light, or rapid cycle.

This bread may be prepared on a timed cycle.

Chocolate Swirl Bread

This is bliss.

It's a good idea to know how long the last (or only) knead is on your bread machine. For this recipe, the chocolate chips should be added about three minutes before the end of the last kneading. It's all right if you put them in earlier, of course, but if you want the rich chocolate swirls, instead of a uniform chocolate bread, put the chips in at the end. Occasionally I've forgotten to add them before it stops kneading, and have had complete success in taking the dough out of the machine (without pushing stop!), working the chips in by kneading by hand for a couple of minutes, then dropping the dough back in to finish rising and baking.

One more caution: this makes a short, dense loaf that is moist in the middle. It won't rise much.

1/3 c heavy cream	2 c bread flour
1/3 c buttermilk	3 T sugar
1 egg, room temperature	1 t cinnamon
3 T butter or margarine,	1 t salt
room temperature	2 t yeast
1/4 c chopped nuts, optional	1/2 c chocolate chips

Add the ingredients to your machine, except the chocolate chips, according to the manufacturer's instructions. Add the chocolate chips at the indicator beep, or 3 minutes before the end of the final kneading.

Use a regular, light, or rapid bread cycle.

Sweet Nut Bread (Dairy-Free)

You can use either crunchy or smooth peanut butter for this recipe.

1 c water

1/2 c peanut butter

2 c bread flour

1/2 c granulated sugar

1/4 c light brown sugar, packed

2 T unsalted peanuts

2 T unsalted pecans

1 t salt (or less if you're using a salty peanut butter)

1 T (3 scant t) yeast

Add the ingredients to your machine according to the manufacturer's instructions.

Bake on a regular, light, or rapid cycle

This can also be prepared on a timed cycle.

Apple Cherry Bread

*This is a variation on a pie recipe that won first place
at a county fair and it's wonderful!*

1/2 c water	1 t salt
1/4 c milk	2 T sugar
1/3 c applesauce	2 t yeast
2 T butter or margarine	1/2 c chopped fresh cherries,
1/2 t almond extract	or 1/3 c dried (cut in half, if
1/2 t vanilla extract	large)
1 t cinnamon	1/3 c dried apple pieces (cut,
1 t grated orange rind	if large)
2 c bread flour	

Add the ingredients to your machine according to the manufacturer's
instructions.

Bake on a regular/white, light, or rapid cycle.

Italian Chocolate Bread

If it is impractical for you to add the chocolate chips during the 3-5 minutes before the end of the last knead, you may add them earlier but they will be thoroughly incorporated into the bread and it will be slightly more dense.

3/4 c + 3 T milk

3 egg yolks

4 T butter or margarine

2 c bread flour, divided

4 T sugar

2 t brown sugar

1/3 c Dutch processed cocoa

1/2 c chocolate chips

1/2 t salt

1 T brown sugar

2–3 t yeast

Put the milk and buttermilk into a saucepan and bring it to a boil. Add 1/2 cup of the bread flour and stir into a thick paste. Let the mixture cool to room temperature, then put it in the bread machine pan.

Add the remaining ingredients, except the chocolate chips.

Add the chocolate chips 3-5 minutes before the end of the last kneading cycle.

Bake on a light or sweet bread cycle.

Colonial Sweet Bread

This is a very old recipe, mildly sweet,
and good for just about everything.

3/4 c + 3 T milk	1/4 c corn meal
1 T butter or margarine	1 t salt
3 T molasses	2 t sugar
2 c bread flour	2–3 t yeast

Add the ingredients to your machine according to the manufacturer's instructions.

Bake on a regular, light, or rapid cycle.

Russian Black Bread (Dairy-Free)

Here's another old world favorite made beautifully in the new-world invention of the bread machine!

1 c + 2 T water

3 T molasses

1 T cider vinegar

2 T butter or margarine

1/2 oz. unsweetened baking
   chocolate

1 c bread flour

1 c rye flour

1/2 c whole wheat flour

1 t instant coffee

1 t salt

1 T caraway seeds

1/4 t fennel seeds

1 T sugar

3 t yeast

Place the water, molasses, butter or margarine, vinegar, and baking chocolate in a small saucepan over medium heat, stirring until thoroughly mixed. Cool to room temperature.

Add the above mixture to the bread machine pan, followed by the remaining ingredients.

Bake on a regular cycle.

Cocoa Peanut Bread

*This is a slightly sweet bread, which can be used for sandwiches
or as a decadent snack with butter.*

*I like to add the peanuts right before the end of the knead, so they stay
intact. Occasionally, I've waited too long and had to take the dough
out of the pan (making sure to leave the pan securely
in the machine or it will re-set) and kneaded
the nuts in by hand.*

1 c milk	1/4 c Dutch processed cocoa
1 egg	1/2 c sugar
1 t vanilla	1 t salt
2 T butter or margarine	1/4 c unsalted peanuts
2 c bread flour	2–3 yeast

Add the ingredients to your machine according to the manufacturer's
instructions. You may add the peanuts at any stage, according to how
crunchy you want your bread.

Use a sweet, regular/white, light, or rapid bread cycle.

Notes

Index

Almond Blue Cheese Loaf, 48
Anadama Bread, *see* New England
 Anadama Bread
Apple Cherry Bread, 138
Apple Walnut Bread, 101
Applesauce Bread, 132
Applesauce Yogurt Bread, 97
Bagel Bread, 80
Banana Oat Bran Bread, 92
Banana Pecan Bread, 64
Banana Wheat Bread, 98
Basil Parmesan Bread, 75
Basil Pepper Feta Loaf, 51
Beer breads, 3, 10, 19, 108, 111, 116, 119
Blueberry Muffin Bread, 65
Bran Chex Bread, 124
Buckwheat Potato Bread, 129
Cashew Gouda Cheese Bread, 82
Champagne "Sourdough" Bread, 18
Champagne and Cheddar Bread, 6
Cheddar Dill Bread, 107
Cheese breads, 6, 11, 19, 41, 50, 51, 52,
 53, 56, 57, 81, 82, 84, 85, 86, 89, 91,
 107, 108, 111, 114, 117, 119, 121, 122
Chips n' Beer Bread, 116
Chocolate Almond Bread, 29
Chocolate breads, 16, 20, 29, 30, 32, 34,
 67, 77, 136, 139, 142
Chocolate Chip Cocoa Bread, 20
Chocolate Oatmeal Bread, 16
Chocolate Spice Rum Babka, 32
Chocolate Swirl Bread, 136
Cinnamon Chip Bread, 36
Cinnamon Cream Bread, 33
Cinnamon Nut Bread, 25
Cocoa Peanut Bread, 142
Colonial Sweet Bread, 140
Cornmeal Herb Bread, 76
Craisin Oatmeal Bread, 31
Cranberry Orange Bread, 23
Cranberry Pumpkin Bread, 130

Cream and Cheese Bread, 114
Cream Cheese Spread, 61
Crunchy Peanut Butter and Honey
 Bread, 93
Dairy-free breads, xiii, 3, 12, 15, 17, 25,
 27, 28, 31, 43, 54, 55, 58, 59, 64, 66,
 79, 80, 83, 88, 92, 93, 99, 116, 120, 128,
 130, 137
Dark Cocoa Bread, 30
Dark Pumpernickel, 128
Dill Bread, 41
Double Cheese Wheat Bread, 110
Double Mustard Onion Beer Bread, 10
Easter breads, 60, 62
Eggs, use of, xii, 4, 32
English Muffin Bread, 123
Farmer's Beer Bread, 119
Finnish Easter Bread, 60
Flour, types of, xii, xiv, 36
French Country Bread, 109
French Sweet Bread with Rum Butter, 35
Fruit breads, x, 9, 22, 23, 24, 25, 26, 28,
 31, 35, 60, 64, 65, 69, 70, 92, 94, 98,
 100, 102, 103, 113, 130, 132, 134, 138
Fruit and Cereal Bread, 113
Garlic Butter Bread, 43
Golden Egg Bread, 4
Golden Raisin Loaf, 28
Grandma's Home-Baked White Bread, 73
Greek Easter Bread, 62
Greek Feta Bread, 84
Gruyère Cheese Bread, *see* "Smells
 Sooooo Good" Gruyère Cheese Bread
Herbs, use of, xiii, 76, 83
Holiday Chocolate Mint Bread, 34
Honey Feta Bread, 89
Honey Mustard Bread, 44
Hoska, *see* Swedish Hoska
Hot Hot Hot Jalapeño Bread, 7
Hot Stuff Cajun Bread, 54
Indian Molasses Bread, 40

Instant Potato Bread, 118
Irish Stout Bread, 108
Italian Peasant Bread, 39
Italian Chocolate Bread, 139
Italian Spice Bread, 58
King's Ransom Bread, 52
Lemon Poppyseed Bread, 102
Light Raspberry Bread, 69
Light Rye with Cheddar and Fennel, 11
Light Wheat Ricotta Bread, 57
Lora Brody's Challah, 127
Macadamia Nut Bread, 99
Maple Oatmeal Breakfast Bread, 27
Mexicali Beer Bread, 3
Milk and Honey Bread, 90
Mocha Cream Bread, 67
Multi-Berry Yogurt Bread, 134
New England Anadama Bread, 112
1950's Kitchen Bread, 47
Nut breads, 9, 22, 24, 29, 35, 48, 60, 62, 64, 82, 103, 120, 121, 136, 137, 142
Nutella Bread, 66
Oatmeal breads, 8, 15, 16, 17, 27, 31, 52, 65, 77, 90, 94, 108, 117
Oat O's Cereal Bread, 8
Oatmeal Molasses Bread, 15
Peanut Butter Cap'n Crunch Bread, 63
Pecan and Raisin Wheat Bread, 24
Pecan Peach Bread, 103
Peppery Garlic Bread, 85
Pizza Al Formaggio, 49
Provençal Garlic Bread, 83
Raisin Bran Bread, 70
Ranch Bread, 87
Rich Dinner Roll Bread, 46
Rosemary Onion Bread, 59
Rosemary-Olive Wheat Bread, 74
Rum-Soaked Currant Bread, 21
Russian Black Bread, 141
Rye breads, 11, 12, 120, 128, 141
Rye Crisps Cracker Loaf, 120
Sally Lunn Bread, 78
Savory Italian Dinner Bread, 81
Savory Olive Bread, 45
Secret Ingredient Chocolate Bread, 77

Semi-Wheat Sally Lunn, 14
Semolina Corn Bread, 5
Sesame Tahini Bread, 17
Sharp Cheddar Bread, 50
"Smells Soooo Good" Gruyère Cheese Bread, 91
Sour Cream Onion and Dill Bread, 125
South Carolina Rice Bread, 13
Spiced Cream Bread, 133
Spiced Rum After Dinner Bread, 135
Spiced White Bread, 42
Strawberry Yogurt Bread, 100
Substitutions, xii, xiii, 5, 24, 25, 31, 47, 48, 53, 64, 80, 102, 111, 130
Sun-Dried Tomato Pizza Bread, 86
Sun-Dried Tomato Polenta Bread, 88
Swedish Hoska, 9
Sweet Crunch Cereal Bread, 131
Sweet Orange Bread, 26
Sweet Nut Bread, 137
Sweet Tropical Bread, 94
Tangy Rye Bread, 12
Tarragon Bread, 53
Tender Wheat Bread, 127
Texas Beer Bread, 19
Tex-Mex Beer 'n' Cheese Bread, 111
Toasted Sesame Bread, 55
Traditional Jewish Challah, 68
Triple Whammy Buttermilk Gorgonzola and Cheddar Bread, 117
Triple Cheese Bread, 122
Troubleshooting, xii, xiii, xiv, , 10, 29, 32, 41, 86, 94, 136
Tuscan Rosemary Bread, 79
Walnut Bread, 121
Walnut Date Bread, 22
Whole Wheat Sour Cream Bread, 115
Wisconsin Dairyland Bread, 56
Yeast, xi, xiv
Yogurt breads, 69, 97, 100, 134
Zucchini Bisque, 96
Zucchini Bisque 'n' Bread, 95